What Does a
LIBRARY MEDIA
SPECIALIST Do?

Winston Garrett

PowerKiDS press

Published in 2015 by The Rosen Publishing Group, Inc.
29 East 21st Street, New York, NY 10010

First Edition

Editor: Norman D. Graubart
Book Design: Colleen Bialecki
Photo Research: Katie Stryker

Photo Credits: Cover Kathy Dewar/E+/Getty Images; p. 5 Cynthia Farmer/Shutterstock.com; p. 6 Shalom Ormsby/Blend Images/Getty Images; p. 9 Looking Glass/Blend Images/Getty Images; p. 10 Ryan McGinnis/Flickr/Getty Images; p. 13 andresrimaging/iStock/Thinkstock; p. 14 Digital Vision/Photodisc/Getty Images; p. 17 Blend Images/Shutterstock.com; p. 18 wavebreakmedia/Shutterstock.com; p. 21 Ingram Publishing/Thinkstock; p. 22 Courtesy of The Historical Society of Glastonbury, Connecticut.

Publisher's Cataloging Data

Garrett, Winston.
What does a library media specialist do? / by Winston Garrett — first edition.
p. cm. — (Jobs in my school)
Includes index.
ISBN 978-1-4777-6546-3 (library binding) — ISBN 978-1-4777-6549-4 (pbk.) — ISBN 978-1-4777-6550-0 (6-pack)
1. School libraries — United States — Juvenile literature. 2. School librarians — United States — Juvenile literature. I. Title.
Z675.S3 W56 2015
027.8—d23

Manufactured in the United States of America

CPSIA Compliance Information: Batch #WS14PK4: For Further Information contact Rosen Publishing, New York, New York at 1-800-237-9932

CONTENTS

People borrow books at the **library**.

Borrowing books is free!

7

Books are due on the **due date**.

9

America's biggest library is
the Library of Congress.

Library media specialists run the library.

They also teach reading.

They are helpful!

They are also called librarians.

They use the **Dewey Decimal System** to sort books. Melvil Dewey came up with it.

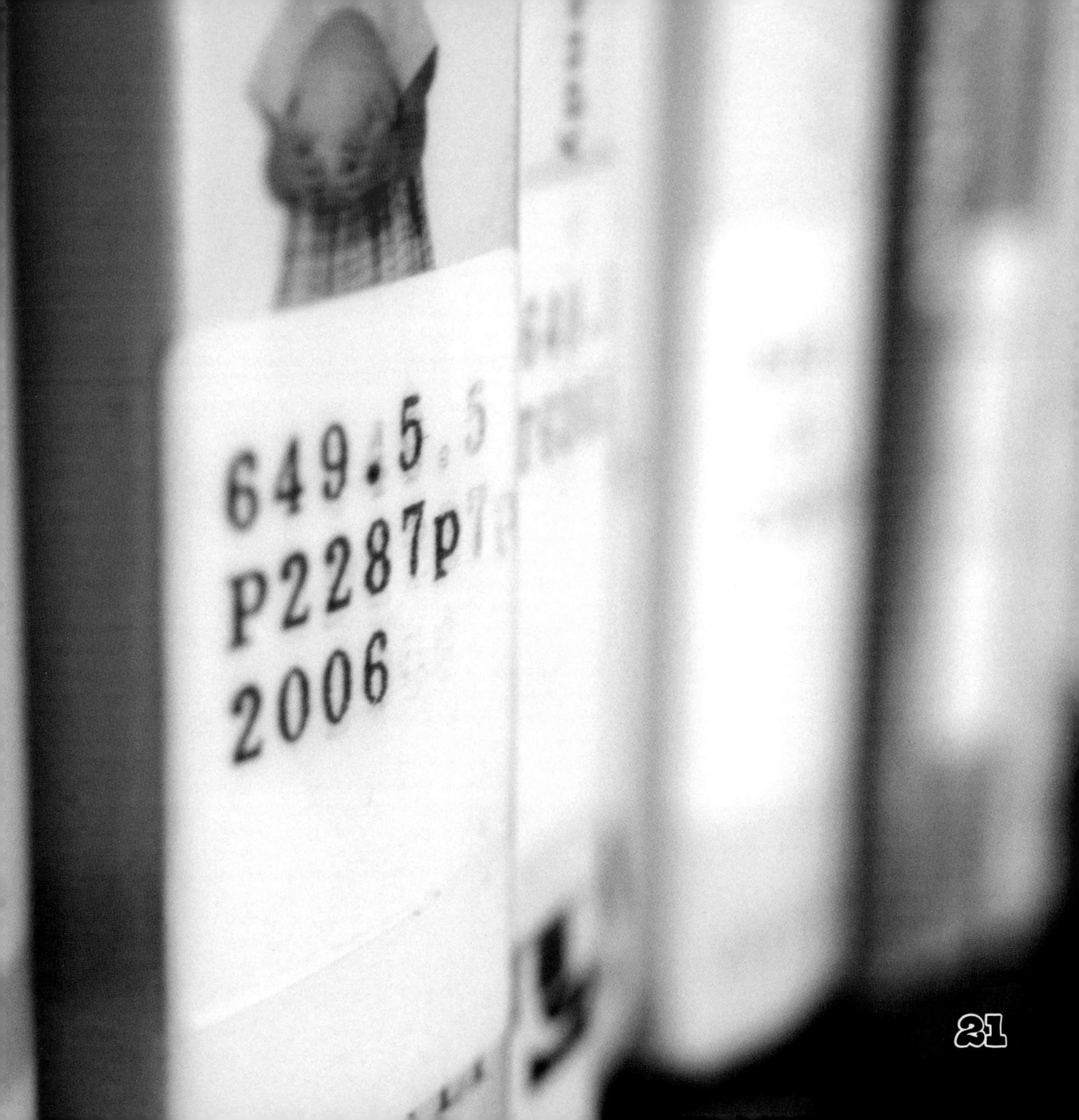
649.5
P2287p
2006

22

Mary Kingsbury was the first trained school librarian.

WORDS TO KNOW

Dewey Decimal System

due dates

library

WEBSITES

Due to the changing nature of Internet links, PowerKids Press has developed an online list of websites related to the subject of this book. This site is updated regularly. Please use this link to access the list: www.powerkidslinks.com/josc/libr/

INDEX